FELTBOARD REVIVAL

Chris Wolfe

Copyright © 2012 Christopher Wolfe
All rights reserved.
ISBN: 0615591809
ISBN-13: 978-0615591803

Branch Hill Publications
P.O. Box 83
Readsboro, Vermont
05350

'Consider this the feltboard revival,
A time to get back to covering up the honest truth.'
~ Chris Wolfe

Table of Contents

Basics
- *The Student*
- *Thunder is a Single Father*
- *Scalpels and Samurai*
- *The Problem. The Answer.*

- *Why I Left the English Department*
- *City That Care Forgot*
- *Only Natural*
- *Seventones*

The Languages
- *El Ojo Aqua*
- *Chateau De Coeur*
- *Phosgraphe Parousia*
- *Ubuntu*
- *Balancé*

Sidenotes
- *Letters to Future Love*
- *Double Letter Score Memories*

The Wilderness
- *Grapes and Salt*
- *They Came for Me*
- *Evening in the Cove*

Glass and Paper and Gasoline
- *The Girl with the Glass Heart*
- *Glass Hearts and Diamonds*
- *Not a Gasoline Heart. Promise.*
- *Diamond, Dream of Diamonds*

Table of Contents continued,

<u>Lent</u>
- *3/30*
- *4/30*
- *5/30*
- *6/30*
- *9/30*
- *11/30*
- *14/30*
- *15/30*
- *16/30*
- *18/30*
- *23/30*
- *24/30*
- *26/30*
- *27/30*
- *30/30*

<u>References and Citations</u>
- *Book*
- *Star-crossed Symphony*
- *Haunted*

<u>Dedications</u>
- *A Vendetta with Keats*
- *Keats Redux*

<u>Appendix</u>
- *Thrift Store*
- *Ink*
- *Writer's Block*

Basics

"Truth had been a weapon. It was about time.
I had said the things only dark rooms
 and notebook paper had heard and seen admissions of."
~ Chris Wolfe, *Carpe Diem, Diamonds, And Doorways*

The Student

Crossing the courtyard
like he had an obligation on the other side,
bearing the burden of at least four authors,
the messenger bag mark of his Finals crucifixion.
Dead Week had been his Passion,
a foreshadowing of his fate after being interrogated by his Pharisee professors,
paid off by a Judas tuition.

The face was rugged.
The alarm set for his five o'clock shadow had been the victim of snooze buttons.
Heavy guitar strings and poems about celestial bodies performed a concert to his right ear,
Stealing away thought processes that created action movie fight scenes between classes.
The left ear remains open.
Cautiously guarding for greetings from other diploma-seeking prophets,
off to regurgitate divine textbook messages of either salvation or damnation,
the realization of which not theirs,
but rather the amount of black dots properly placed in a color-by-number answer sheet.

His key chain at this side rang like Legion's chains with every step.
The voices of one-thousand flash card answers spoke in his mind at the same time.
Open wounds from arithmetic floggings and literary Roman Guards
and each step towards the fourth floor was a step to Golgotha.

Thunder is a Single Father

I fall asleep to thunderstorms,
learning from them subconsciously
how they rule the world.
Lightning is a failure.
He strikes, fizzles out, and leaves.
All quicker than your eyes
could blink. But
Thunder, he and I are friends.
He mentors me in
the ways of passive ruling:
wait until Lightning has failed.
And if he's far away,
wait longer.
Then when no one is looking
shake the very foundations
of the world, rattle souls,
and be heard for longer
than any timekeeper can count.

Lightning is a show off,
flashy and narcissistic.
'Look at me! Look at me!'
Always interrupting while
we are trying to speak.
Thunder shares stories of experience
about how he was there for
the voice of God, and
he'd never been so afraid in
his entire existence.
Thunder had just nearly
finished teaching his lessons.
'Look at me! Look at me!'
Lightning interrupted.
An upset child sprawled
across the sky,
kicking and screaming,

Poem continues ...

Thunder is a Single Father, continued

'Look at me! Look at me!'
Knocking over trees and
setting fire to mountains.

Thunder had enough. He
picked up the crying
Child, roared as many
final goodbyes as Lightning's
infantile cries.
Even as they left and
walked away from my
home, I could hear
Thunder shouting comforting words,
only scaring Lightning into
crying somewhere else.
Finally, it was silent,
but elsewhere Thunder is teaching
with his bratty kid in tow.

Scalpels and Samurai

Skin rose red flush,
minor allergic or heartbeat
speed up, unsure.
Doctors can't diagnose the
obvious symptoms, while
simple advice tells me
that sympathy and sensitivity
to your own heart
is over halfway to
capturing it …

… and holding on
to the idea of life's journey.
Where does your heart lie
on this path I walk?
Are you one mile,
three miles, or a marathon's worth?
Running's not something I do
but I've run for twenty-three so far
and if I have to run the next
three then I will. But I'm hitting
the wall waiting and it's not
that I'm impatient but,

when you had a burst of
energy and grasp onto
that little cup of
water fighting for every last drop,
it gets hard to keep fighting
and not just give up …

… and retreat and run.
Every day is a new battle.
Yours is the only love
that's ever made my heart
and mind fight like samurai.

Poem continues …

Scalpels and Samurai, continued.

Springtime war cries in a field.
An orchard of trees.
Japanese cherry blossoms
fall. Balance of beauty and
battle. And finally I have
to step in and stop the
warriors before they
strike the princess and
everyone loses …

… but everyone wins.
They remind me it's not
important. Well, it is.
But it's not. Heartbeats,
faster and slower at the same time,
are a fatal heart attack.
So no wonder when you
decide someone, something,
spirit, body, mind,
is so gorgeous that
'drop-dead' is the only
adjective a writer can find.

The Problem. The Answer.

I've been writing this since before the sun got here
since the stars said their good nights
since the moon ran again
with more of the sun's stolen light

I've been writing this since before you were born
since your own parents' honeymoon
since you were barely an afterthought of their love
with palm trees and ocean breezes cheering them on.

The moon was high in the sky and
there we sat for our turn.
Adrenaline pumping like a red light turning green.

My own body told me lies.
It pushed and pulled
and pushed and pulled.
Like a primary school fist fight
at 'high noon' three P.M. recess times.

The problem was that you weren't there
and whether or not that made it easier
I wasn't sure.

The problem was that I'd seen the moon more times
than I'd seen your face or the sun this week.
As to which one I missed more,
I wasn't sure.

But like a three-part harmony therapy session
I stood up and let those burdens ring out.
Ring out like I'd just punched out Mike Tyson in the third round
Ring out like I'd just scored a 36 on the ACT
Ring out like I'd just asked the girl of my dreams to marry me
and she'd said yes before I'd ever pulled the ring out.

Poem continues ...

The Problem. The Answer. continued.

By the end of the night,
they'd all heard the stories
of heroes and hearts and
heartbreaks and hope.

The only problem was that I'd seen the sun this morning as it rose
and I knew which one I missed more.

Why I Left the English Department

Today's Assignment:
'In 250 words or less, describe her the best.'

So I sit here and toil over these instructions.
'Two Hundred and Fifty? Is that all I have?
To describe everything about you and why I feel it?
Why gravity itself stopped and let go when you entered the room?
Why the foundations of the Earth shook when you asked me my name?'
I hit the delete key a thousand and one times.
Never once was I able to fit it all in just this painful limitation.
'Two Hundred and Fifty? You must be crazy.
Did the world not move for you too? You must know what I'm talking about.
How can you ask me a question if you don't know the answer yourself?'

So I started typing, forcing myself to hold you back from them.

Like a two hundred and fifty foot leash, you expect me to explain?
We know I will run full speed and at the end of this leash
I will hang myself on the final word.
Fight as hard as I possibly can to two hundred fifty and one.

I will run circles around this lot.
I will find ways to deviate your rules.
I will be this place's worst nightmare.
I will be this building's savior.
I will show them the way to two hundred fifty and one.

'Sorry, son,' he says. 'You failed for breaking the rules.'
And so I left here because
It's a shame you couldn't allow two hundred fifty and one.
Maybe then I tell her how much I love

City That Care Forgot

It had been years since the music played here.
The soul had left this place. The spirit evacuated long before the people did.
Washed away along with hope and houses.

A few notes began to play.
She said her love was in New Orleans. His heart was a wild hurricane.
The last had left devastation. This one would bring realization.

Open mic nights brought back hope.
Soon the sounds of 'NOLA jazz' filled the streets.
Soon the people of 'NOLA spirit' did too.

Noise and confetti were joyous return.
She found her love in New Orleans. His hope was a stable foundation.
Building up futures in new houses and hearts.

Only Natural

This music is my medicine, my life.
From this first beat, the blood starts pumping
Snare become systolic, bass becomes diastolic.
They try and tell me to calm down,
But this song of mine plays at 140 over lungs and chest.

And when the cymbals crash, it's me holding my breath.
The hairs on my skin stand straight as the strings on your guitars.
I could rub them together like a couple hundred violins playing at once.

This body of mine is the orchestra by now.
My ribs are the chairs of the concert halls,
Each breath opens and closes these doors to new listeners.

Sometimes I speak
And you can hear their notes crawling up,
Past my lips and into the air and just maybe they will be heard

By the people standing outside longing to get in,
By the beggars on the street corners,
By the homeless in the alleys between here and the bars.

So for that I refuse to quiet,
So for that my music may become your music.

Seventones

It was raining as I dialed the seven numbers
that would connect me to you.
You just rang busy,
as I expected.
But decided to call again.

Seven tones later I found you on the other end.
In no mood to talk, but you listened anyway.
I told you about the world and
you told me about the sky and
together we talked for hours about how
all things were still in their color.

Lightning began to ring outside,
bringing with it the shock of percussion
whose simple goal was to interrupt us.
I wouldn't let it, but it insisted.
Lights went out, buzz of power stopped.
Lightning was jealous that it wasn't the only
power that night. So he killed the other and left
us in the dark.

But we persisted, persevered, pressed on,
talked long into the night about our life,
but just as I was ready to say . . . .
The batteries died too, and Lightning and Thunder
mocked me for their deeds.

They knew you'd never get to hear me speak again.

The Languages

"... but I am not the gasoline heart anymore. I am the abstract prophet speaking in Pentecostal tongues. Just try and tempt me. I am not weak anymore."

~ Chris Wolfe, *Stolen*

El Ojo Aqua

Your eyes are oceans
Save your life jackets for someone who cares not to drown in them
Save your boats for someone who doesn't want to swim around in them
Those flecks of green are the islands within you
Lush tropic beauty, wash me ashore your white sandy beaches
Deserted islands with so much to discover
Allow me to stay here for a while
Allow me to linger in them
Find these secrets you hide among the trees
The secrets hiding behind your gaze

Do not turn your eyes away
Rescue me from these untouched shores
Leave me here to survive on my own
To dig up the treasures you've left here

Do not close your eyes
When you blink it is sun setting on this isle
My connection lost. Night time
Your eyes' opening is the sunrise to a new morning
A new five second day in which I get to explore this place again

Do not cry
Your tears are a new tropic rainstorm
A hurricane to toss up this paradise
Wipe them away, these drops of salt water causing high tide
Allow me to sail away on calm seas
Your eyes are oceans

Chateau De Coeur

Your heart is a castle, a fortress.
Each slighted gaze just another watchtower you've obstructed.
Like a heartache Trojan horse, I send in honesty and hope you will also see I care.

I wish I was strong enough to break down the walls you put up.
But I don't want to be careless and break down your walls
So the next empty words break in and break your heart.

Why is it that we battle?
Or are we even at all?
Is it my heart that is the castle
And you are just too scared to come in?

Phosgraphe Parousia

I have seen visions of photographs that have yet to be taken.
I wish you could have seen yourself.
The gown you pick for our wedding,
You can't be more beautiful.
I apologize for seeing you before our wedding day,
But I think just this once, the superstitions will let it slide.

I have seen the decorations you pick out.
You do such a great job.
I wonder how stressed out we will be.
I do not worry because I have seen your smile next to mine.
Our families look as happy as we are.
Just wait until you see who we pick as our best man and maid of honor.

You remind me of happy maritimes we learned to swim
While the satellites illuminate our way.
I will not yet share who you are
But look forward to sharing this with you,
Along with vows and a ring,
When we live out these Polaroids.

Ubuntu

I didn't realize how much I needed you.
All of you.
Without you, I felt exiled in my hometown.
Sitting in my room, I waited for your return
Daily I walked back to your community.
We talked, we prayed,
We argued, we cried.
I kissed you goodbye.
And exile met me like a welcome mat,
A warm cup of tea and a safety blanket.
Refugee imprisoned me in quiet comfort.
Every day for a week, it was painful routine.
I didn't exist for twenty hours.
And by the time you returned
I had only lived a day.
When I laid eyes on you today,
I met you and existence on the welcome mat,
A warm cup of tea and a safety blanket.

Balancé

Who saves the poets?
We've been trapped in our heads and dreams
Since the pencil first hit paper.
Abstraction and Delusion,
Dreams and Absolution.

I must admit I have scars you've yet to see.
Even now. After everything …
I hope you stick around long enough to find out.
Just long enough. Then do as you please.
Break me down easily, or stick around longer.

Who saves the poets?
You dance about on tip-toes and half-notes,
Learned skills and empathy, heal.
Ballerina steps on a glass floor
Careful not to break.

Sidenotes

"The sad part is what happens when I find your future."
~ Chris Wolfe, *Stolen*

Letters To Future Love

'… I prayed for you again today. I don't know what you're going through, but I hope it's not too much trouble. are you in school? are you working? How's your family? tell them hi for me … well, if you knew me, then they'd know me and I'd want them to know I cared about them too …'

'… realized today I don't know who you are, but met a few people over the last few weeks who could overtake your spot in my heart. unless you are one of them. in which case, I'm happy to have met you. I hope I wasn't too annoying. I'm pretty new at this whole thing. I don't know your likes or dislikes, or your hobbies. I hope it isn't your birthday and I forgot to tell you happy birthday. Well … happy birthday if it is …'

'… and it was late at night and I was singing all these lovey-dovey songs I'd never even given the time of day to on the radio. I hope you appreciate all this singing I do for you. I don't hear it but I have you in mind when I'm singing out loud with windows down. some of my friends even laugh at me to find that I knew the words to that song, but it's the only one that really reminds me of you. well, I think it reminds me of you even if I haven't met you yet. what kind of music do you like? what kind of movies are you into? because I hope to take you out sometime for a movie or a concert, but I'd have to meet you or know you or really know what you wanted to do that made you happy …'

'… someone asked me if I loved you, if I paid any attention to you or knew that I knew you, then I'd know what to do. what to say to you when I met you one day. or what to say to you to let you know now. sorry, I probably wouldn't tell you that I loved you. either because my friends are crazy, or because I got lost, until finally we were at the corner table of a restaurant and I could speak to you in private. or until I knew for sure myself. I'm not a confident man, which probably leads to why I've not met you yet. come to think of it, I've probably met you a million times and just didn't have the guts to say 'hello.' so be patient with me. I'll come around one day. until then, just be patient.

Poem continues ...

Letters to Future Love, continued.

you can even date a few guys until then. I'm not jealous. how else are you gonna find out who you are, what you want in someone, and all those things? I'll probably even screw up a few times and date the wrong girls a few times too. please don't be jealous or upset. a few of them will probably lie and tell me they are 'you.' that somehow they are 'the one' and I'll probably fall for it too. even still, I remind you that in the end it's me and you. and that keeps me faithful and moving forward. I've been playing scavenger hunts for hearts to finally find you so give me some time, because I never know when I'm going to finally stumble upon you …'

'… think I had a dream about you today. I think God himself was there trying to play matchmaker and put us together. kinda like Adam getting a rib taken out and God creating Eve, I think He must have taken out half my ribcage because you were so amazingly beautiful that I couldn't possibly believe the happiness it caused. I catch myself writing notes to you in my sleep, like somehow I'm gonna be able to mail them through whatever connections my mind has to this dreamworld and you're gonna wake up and find them in your mailbox that morning and read these sweet words from some secret admirer. I hope you don't find my being so forward uncomfortable … I've spent quite a few times writing letters to you or saying prayers for you so that no matter who you are, God will take care of you and I'm ready to know if I know you yet …'

'… just wanted you to know you already make me happy. if we've met, I think we'll make amazing friends. and if we've yet to meet, I think we'll make amazing friends. I doubt you'll ever receive any of these letters, but it's my hope that you still feel like you've read them after we've talked and spent some time together …'

'see you soon ..? or later ..? or tomorrow? or in five minutes? or from across the room when I look up from this letter … take care of yourself … don't get into too much trouble … and most importantly …

… hurry up and let me find you.'

Double Letter Score Memories

Call it boredom, Scrabble tiles and an empty board.

      'LANGUOR' : a word score of 61 points and a definition to match the mood.
      lan*gour [lang-ger] - noun: a lack of emotional interest or physical strength.

      The word put me ahead by 25 points of the opponent who didn't exist. Use of six letters left me with only one and, drawing more tiles, I pulled the tiles that spelled a familiar name. I don't know that I smirked or sneered, but my reaction to God was one of humor.

      'You are funny,' I chuckled as I wagged my finger in the air, as if to shame Him for his irony, an irony in itself.

      I got up from the table and allowed my rival the space he needed to choose his next word. I told him that I'd be back in a moment, leaving to pick up a drink and asking if he wanted something while I was out. And not to change anything on the board, of course.

      No answer. I assumed he was deep in thought.

      I grabbed my keys from the table and the overcoat on the hanger. As I avoided the icy patches on the steps, I guided my hand down the cold railing like a kindergartener and a chain link fence. Instead of getting in the car and starting it up, I began walking to the store, dodging the sky as it fell. The sidewalks and streets were empty except for a few city trucks out salting the roads. They'd salted the sidewalks before it ever got cold, assuming the worst. The sodium chunks crunched with every step. At the corner of the third block, I stopped and lifted the hood from my jacket, pressing the button to begin the electrical processes to get me across this empty street.

      Poem continues ...

Double Letter Score Memories, continued.

  I must have stumbled into the downtown district, because only here were you going to hear music of the Big Band era, especially when no one is around. I wasn't entirely sure, but I thought I could hear Ol' Blue Eyes singing some song about sunshine and moonlight and I wondered if he knew we were in a deficit of both on this old downtown streets. Would he be okay knowing how his song was being thrown around so easily?

  Inside the store, I walked back to the coolers and found that holding it open while I decided was actually warming me up compared to the bitter cold outside. I grabbed a Cherry Coke and a large bottle of what these people like to call 'green tea.' I paid the lady at the register with a few crinkled dollar bills and old grimy quarters. Strangely, I got a sneer and a wink, finding an inkling of bipolar in her advance. I grabbed my plastic bag and let the single bell ring be my answer to her question.

  It smelled like cherries and old snow. Sweet and sour. Sometimes I wonder how much the world has the same smells. My mind beat me home, seeing the seven letters that spelled out the name. The sweet taste of the cherries was only a relic, an artifice.

  Just ten minutes later, I was already back home. My bottle of memories half gone and this other bottle of misjudged liquid waiting to do its job. 'I'm back,' I yelled through the house.

  No answer. I assumed he was deep in thought.

  I walked back into the room and looked down at the board. He had played it and left me for a while.

  PARAMOUR played off the 'R' in LANGUOR:

  A word score of 62 and he had used all of his letters to spell it.

               Poem continues ...

Double Letter Score Memories, continued.

      I bet he smirked when he'd seen he'd one-upped me in every regard. I looked down at my letters and used them to spell out the name. He'd never allow it to stand, but I had to play it. My only argument is your name is its own purpose.

We Only Sleep When It Rains

We only sleep when it rains,
each aquatic drop carries down
a new word to the story,
the lightning and thunder fight to make nightmares.
The windowsill filters out the nonsense.

Dreams came in the day.
She must have been a part of them.
She appeared with the sun at her back,
looking up from my book to greet her.
She extended a hand and a smile.

Eyes of green, but she had contacts of blue.
Wind blew through hair like the night sky.
I shook her hand and we exchanged names.
As I held out a hand to cover the sun,
I recognized a face I'd never seen before.

It only rains when we sleep.
Our insomnia at fault for the droughts.
Our sleeping-in at fault for the monsoons.
Our nightmares at fault for the severe thunderstorms.
Our tossing and turning at fault for the tornadoes.

I chased her up the stairs,
grabbed an ankle before she got to the top.
She slid back down, sat on a step above me,
hung two arms down over my shoulders.
A kiss on the wrist. A kiss on the back of the hand.

143s. ILYs. I<3Us.
Whatever you call them, we exchanged those words.
Music played lightly from two rooms over.
Silently I shuffled my hand into my pocket,
slipped the gold band over her finger.

Poem continues ...

We Only Sleep When It Rains, continued.

They say dreams are gateways to the mind.
They say the eyes are the gateway to the soul.
They say you dream more during an electrical storm.
They say it's good luck if it rains on your wedding day.

The sound of glasses clanging together.
The toast from the best man.
The veil had been lifted.
The cake cut and sliced.
The bouquets tossed.

Held her over the threshold as we entered the door,
still in our suits and dresses.
Palm trees outside our windows.
Skin perfect, a few freckles that mapped the constellations.
Laughing, awkward, family, silly, love, bed, us, I

Passed out, any number of storms or showers.
Nightmares make for interesting nights.
A lack of roofs and tree branches for our bad dreams,
sunny days changed into maelstroms.
It only rains when we sleep.

Flowers and tears in each eye.
Candles lit. Standing still on their guard posts.
I may have had the wings but she was the angel.
They held a door open for her,
I held open a door for her.

They took her and lowered her beneath their feet.
I took her and raised her back out.
I'd waited on her for 6 years.
I appeared with the sun at my back.
I extended a hand and a smile.

Poem continues ...

We Only Sleep When It Rains, Continued.

The showers came to an end.
The dreams came to an end.
I don't know if it was a nightmare or not.
Dreams come and go every night.
We only sleep when it rains.

The Wilderness

"I got something important back.
I intend to capture it like fireflies in a mason jar."
~ Chris Wolfe, *10/30*

Grapes and Salt

Just breathe.

I tossed another bottle into the ocean with the same letter I'd copied a hundred times at the Kinko's. At this rate I was either going to get my answer or an arrest for littering or dumping into the ocean. I popped the cork on another bottle of $15 wine and poured it into the sand. It smelled like old grapes and salt. I picked up another letter and brushed the sand off and read the first paragraph:

' … sat no more than 5 feet from me and I can't tell you what's running through my head. I want to tell you how much you mean … to ask you if it's possible ... but for now you remain far away … '

I rolled up the letter and slipped it in the bottle. I thought about how the reader of this message was going to find a red-stained piece of paper with illegible scribble on it. They weren't going to be able to answer my questions any better than I could. I shoved the cork back in the bottle and sealed it water tight, stood up and grabbed the narrow end of the bottle and just as I got ready to launch the bottle, another one washed up at my feet. I was angry, sad, confused. 'Were my bottles not making it far enough out? Were they just washing back up on my shore?' I didn't recognize this one, this was no wine bottle. I dropped my own bottle in the sand and picked up the new one. I wasn't alone tonight. Someone else was questioning.

'… just as afraid as you. I wonder sometimes about the way you look at me ... is it possible that you ... are you waiting for?'

I recognized the handwriting.

They Came For Me

They came out of the water,
Survivors of their own dreams.
Crawled out onto the shore
Just in time to awake during the night.
The moon crossed and danced
Its borrowed beams across the top of the lake.

They came out of the air,
Blindsided by northern winds.
Landed atop the cliffs
Just in time to cover themselves
With their wings and hide
From my sight before they dived.

They came out of the earth,
Plated by dirt and crags of granite and marble.
Rolling out, covered in roots and moss
Just in time to show their eyes glowing green
In the nighttime darkness,
Surrounded by the forest.

They came from the fire,
Embers floating and forming fiery spirits.
Setting fire to the ground at their feet
Just in time for me to watch them
Crawling from my campfire
Smoke and ash hiding their faces.

They came out of the shadows,
Ghostly figures, barely seen as they hide and wait.
Inching closer to my toes
As the fire grew dim and embers glowed.
Placing their hands on my shoulder,
Embracing me with their cold, cold hands.

Poem continues ...

They Came For Me, continued.

I came out of the light,
Six wings ablaze in fire and lightning.
I pulled back my hood to show
Eyes glowing cobalt and a face of thunder.
I told them all to leave, 'tempt me no more.'
I flew away, after 40 days and nights of the same.

Evening in the Cove

This time of year, the trees are all the same color.
Nature itself is teaching us colorblind equality.
It's that kind of green that God creates
So that every flower and blossom is in perfect color theory.
If anyone knows color scheme, it's Him.

Something about this year just
Screams renewal, revival.
Like this year is gonna be the year.
Success. Progress. Love.
It's going to happen this time.

There's healing this time around.
There's strength this time around.
Everything's a little more colorful.
Everything's a little more bright.
Just try and stop me this time.

Glass and Paper and Gasoline

"I want to write a song that sounds like sepia tone."
~Chris Wolfe, *22/30*

The Girl with the Glass Heart

I had a dream that I met a girl with a glass heart.
It was crystal clear and beautiful.
In the light, it separated out the colors of the sun.
Underneath it, all my smallest flaws became magnified so I could identify and fix them.

She walked up to me, smiled up at me, and handed me the glass heart.
Hesitantly said I could take a closer look.

I took the glass heart, held it up in the sunlight.
Smiled at all its refracted colors, held it up and examined the flawless clarity.
It was so spotless. You'd never believe her stories.

About the people who'd halfheartedly tossed the fragile thing about.
Juggled it and misplaced it and lost it.
About the times she'd dropped it herself. Lost trust in such a beautiful fragile thing.

I dared not speak. Afraid to have the glass heart so close.
My own gasoline heart could flicker up and ignite and melt and ruin such clarity.
Nervously, I walked back to the little girl.
I tripped over my own tongue. Stumbled about upon my own words
And the painful words of those closest to her.

I tripped and fell. The glass heart tumbled through the air.
I fell face down, hearing the glass heart fall and crash to the ground.
I dared not look up. Afraid to see the shattered heart and the effects of my carelessness.
Afraid to see the little girl crying, stumbling, scooping up the little pieces.

Poem continues ...

The Girl With The Glass Heart, continued.

As I lay there and cried and mourned the fragile heart, I heard a little voice telling me to get up.
I looked up and was blinded by colors and lights. The little girl held the glass heart above me.
The heart amazingly intact despite my carelessness with it.
She took my hand and pulled me up. Told me not to worry but held the fragile heart a little tighter.

I've not seen the glass heart since. Some say it's been given to another. Held onto tightly by a trusted friend.
I prayed he'd not make the same mistake if he loved it so much more than I.
Such a fragile thing. Such a beautiful thing
Is worth far too much to haphazardly break.

Glass Hearts and Diamonds

Like a traveling museum exhibit
Her and her fragile heart rolled back into town.
Just as I'd remembered them both.

A soul as strong as diamonds
A heart like glass.

With all the stories and lies I'd heard
The first few times felt like
Tip-toeing around a mine field.

But perception isn't reality.
Sometimes glass hearts are diamonds.
Sometimes the best gifts are wrapped in typical packaging.

I wondered how much longer it would be
Until everyone else realized it too.

But does she know?

The tiny crystalline heart,
That so many mistook as made of simple glass,
Was actually a diamond in the rough.

Glass hearts break and shatter
Into a million tiny stars
When you carelessly drop them on the floor.

Only a diamond could have been put through
Such fire and pressure and made it out
Glowing brighter than before.

But does she know?

Poem continues ...

Glass Hearts and Diamonds, continued.

Does she know she carries a diamond heart?
Or does she see only fragile glass too?

With so many facets and colors
How could you mistake this diamond
For a plastic prism?

Can a glass heart
Withstand the heat
Of a fire sparked by carelessness
Of gasoline hearts?

Can a glass heart
Withstand the juggling
And shuffling of the distracted
Half-hearted?

Can a glass heart
Withstand the flimsy
Erasable promises signed
On the lines of paper hearts?

But does she know?

Her diamond heart
The reason why she is
So easily taken in.

The diamond heart
Easily cuts through
Defenses and sees truth.

The diamond heart
Why she only sees value
When others see worthless.

Poem continues ...

Glass Hearts and Diamonds, continued.

But does she know?

Like a traveling museum exhibit,
Her and her diamond heart rolled back into town.
Just as I'd remembered them both.

Diamond, Dream of Diamonds

I once decided to share my dreams.
But they told me that was impossible.
I dream to detach.
But not depressed, to leave.
You go to sleep every night and
I've already seen the glimpses.
Your nightmares hide in your eyes.
Worries and anxiety about badly told stories.
Fiction is troublesome.
Dream of truth.

I once shared my dreams.
But I was told it was impossible.
I dream for diamonds.
Somewhere between guardian angel
And dreamcatcher.
Watch close for a glimmer in your peripheral.
Something too real to be a dream.
Something too dreamlike to be really there.
Catching tears like raindrops and spiderwebs,
Finding diamonds on every capturing strand.
Hero to one. Only one. But
Bad dreams and fiction like disease.

I wake up from a long night
Of holding them back.
Coughing and sputtering.
Filtering fiction from designed dreams.

I dream I dream.
But I was told to wake up.
I dream the impossible.
The only truth was that I wished
To break the cycle.
Diamonds with defects do not shine so well.
So wake up from your own dreams.

Poem continues ...

Diamond, Dream of Diamonds, Continued.

Arise and shine, shine, shine!
Nightmares have no power.
Nightmares are poorly told tales.
The one time I wanted magic answers,
I want for dreams like bedtime stories.
Pop-up picture princesses
In diamond castles and Prince Charmings.
These are real dreams.
These are your dreams.
If nightmares are what plague your nights,
Then I can only promise your dreams will be found in your days.

Lent
'If you knew the battle my heart is having over you,
we'd sign the treaty and start the after party.'
~Chris Wolfe, *8/30*

3/30

I woke up today with a train in my throat.
Five boxes of used matches were scattered in my bed.
The smell of cigars puffed from the engine's stack.

A conductor starts to yell words that sound like an instruction manual
on how to build a table.
Being a man, I decided I didn't need them.

A pastor was on board so we built the table and had communion.
The kitchen was out of bread and wine,
So the waitress brought us bottles of water and a travel catalog
Hoping we may find salvation for a reasonable price,
Or at least a payment plan to pay it off before we died.

4/30

I'd never seen a sky so big.
We sat atop the hill in the backyard of a home I'd lived in since my childhood.
The phases of the moon projected out across the sky
As if they were the points on a compass.
The southern sky laid bare with the new moon phase.
An empty spot where the lack of a satellite was a memorial to the dark nights
Where we'd sat atop the fire tower on top of the mountains that sat behind us.

You and I, we had laid atop that old platform,
Talking about our lives, stories above the tallest trees.
Uniformed men used to sit atop these and keep a look out for wildfires
Tonight watched the headlights of ants and sparks of streetlights flicker in the cities below us.

One day we may go there again.

5/30

My heart is a small bird.
Singing the songs it hears
A slight humming as it pulses out new notes
On a good day it tries to fly away to you like a carrier pigeon
Hoping to bring a small piece of paper
Across town to you.
Yet the bird is trapped inside this cage
And these lungs I use to sing and breathe
Are suffocating and beating up this little thing.
Maybe one day after I die, you will find this small piece of paper
Still attached, sitting in another cage.

6/30

I walked into the Sam's Club hoping they were selling hopes and dreams in bulk
But getting into that place is like I had to be a Freemason or an Illuminati.
Must be because they sell the Secret to Life next to the Holy Grail next to the Budweiser next to the cigarettes.
You must be this tall to ride. You must be this rich to matter.
So I go across the street to the Kmart
And find them on sale and in three different colors.

9/30

'You see that tree over there.'
My grandfather points it out.
The swing on the front porch creaks as I shift my weight.
We planted that when we first moved here.
The tree rings in that tree
Must have as many stories
As my grandfather does.
I'd like to believe he is twice as strong though.

11/30

I saw lightning do something weird today.
It played a cover song on a 12-string guitar.
It cooked a full meal and welcomed me over for lunch after church.
It showed me how to tie my shoe laces,
Start a camp fire,
Bandage a wound.
It folded up a piece of paper and flew an airplane to my feet.
It took me out on a raft and we fished for antique furniture.
Taught me how to scale, filet, and take a nap on it.

14/30

Allow this to sink in
Like a sunburn or tattoo
My biggest mistake will be letting you go
My biggest reward will be up to you.

15/30

This mailbox has been empty for weeks.
Mercury hasn't come to my driveway to drop off some letters.
Stand up the flag.
Leave me some songs.

16/30

A bird fell from the sky.
Its wing clipped by a meteor falling from the ocean.
It sang Frank Sinatra on spring cleaning days,
whistled Louis Armstrong during the summer thunderstorms
and chanted old slave spirituals when the leaves fell.
The lake out in the clearing froze and turned into our ice rink.
By then the bird's wing had mended.
Icarus left on New Year's Day.
I expect to see him again one day.

18/30

It's raining here on the downtown streets.
Patrons from the local cafe are rushing inside from their patio tables.
The beautiful waitress stands strong in the winds
trying to save the umbrella from floating away.
She has a future career as a magical babysitter.
I help her catch it before it becomes a runaway kite
and push her back against the overhang to keep the rain
from drowning her midnight hair.
Handing over Lincoln, I tell her to keep Washington's twins
and with a 'thank you' and a wink,
she walks back inside.

To this day I wake up at night when it rains.

23/30

My bones ache as if there were a storm on the horizon.
There are rainclouds in my muscles and
lightning in my throat.

24/30

These city streetlights are so bright.
Maybe it's the sleep deprivation talking,
but you might be the most beautiful thing
I've ever bumped into waiting for the Blue Line.

I'll meet you here tomorrow.
Same time. Same place.
No words. Just a prayer,
That I'll work up the courage to take the bus home.

26/30

the glass was cold.
Staring outside hoping to see
two lights come up the drive
like fireflies in the summer
a sign of something better on its way.
You breathed on the glass
and drew a bass note
remembering it's part of who I am.
Late at night when I finally made it home
You were asleep on the chair next to the door.
In the morning you woke up
to find another note written from the outside,
completing a sign of what's keeping us together here.

27/30

A part of me just isn't the same anymore.
Traumatizing humility in the face of uncertainty.
I'm not dead but a part of me changed in a moment.
Coming to terms with the hard truth
While ever spinning destruction skips thru the city streets.

30/30

I'm not sure what the future holds anymore.
Everything I thought was written in stone
was a sandcastle house of card boarding houses.
It's only a matter of time until I lose you.
Déjà vu is a way of life around here,
A religion.

References and Citations

"You're always going to be like listening to Big Band on vinyl. You'll always be my favorite but it's nothing like being there in person."

~Chris Wolfe, *2/30*

Book

There is a small leather bound journal
Shuffled underneath my bed
Beside dirty socks and heartbreak --
And heartache, small but so noticeable.
It is the small pea placed by the princess
At the bottom of the book's two hundred and fifty papyrus mattresses.
She is sleeping high upon the pages.

Each night I knit together these literary quilts
And lay another over her to keep her warm.
Yet she tosses and turns the pages all night.

There is a small scrapbook of fables
Shuffled underneath my bed
Beside the dirty pages and coffee stains --
There are tales of a man trying to stay alive,
But every time he opens this book,
His body bleeds out a little more with each line of ink.
His spine is broken a little more with every page that is turned.

The princess, she is still warm.
Safety blanket blank pages, but
I am removing these one at a time.

There is a half-full, half-empty Bible
Shuffled underneath my bed
Beside the glass of water it resembles.
It beckons me to write my own gospel,
But I have no miraculous signs of water and wine,
Only a couple hundred thirsty guests
Longing for me to solve their unquenchable complications.

The princess left long ago,
Knocking over half a glass of red wine,
Dragging my novel bedsheets behind her.

Star-Crossed Symphony
(co-written with Kristina Arrowood)

I sat in the in-between
Drifting from fantasy to consciousness
The blackness around my eyes speckled with colors
Taking shape and dancing to the tune of my own dreams.

They played out to me like orchestra and chorus
Synesthesia-colored harmony with artistic precision
Mona Lisa played from first chair violin and
Soprano sculpted the statue of David
Radiant as sun's reflection on angels' wings.

As dawn breaks, my orchestra pauses
Melody's notes written by laughter
My pulse, the metronome.

Tick tock heartbeat, heartstrings symphony
Empty concert halls were a sign of alarm clock pending
I left the echoes to do their own bidding
As eyes open to new dawn promises of writing songs in the day

Tears mix with words left unspoken
Staining the lyrics of this romantic's anthem
Angels' feathers fall upon unraveling violin strings
The metronome falters.

So silence falls over the day
Each action like out-of-tune piano keys
A lack of lyrics means you never know
A song only the angels' instruments play
A melody that haunts a lover's ear
Played by the damned to empty theater chairs.
At the precipice of heart strings breaking
This heavenly tune becomes 'star-crossed.'

Poem continues ...

Star-Crossed Symphony, continued.

So now a wondering from the very beginning,
Was the statue of David really Romeo pondering
Why Da Vinci's Juliet no longer smiles?
Musician's lack of talent her last drop of poison.

Words ceasing at the lips of lovers
Melody piercing the heart's iniquities
The harmony sacrificed upon this ballad.
 Tick tock heartbeat, and the metronome falters.

Haunted
(co-written with Kristina Arrowood)

I stand
Hands trembling
Because I followed you here,
Or maybe it was there,
Somewhere lost in a dream
Where sun splattered through red and green.
Frigid breezes hide the shaking
Caught in the midst of autumnal daydream.

These trees are full of thoughts I keep forgetting,
The time of year where the buildup of hopeful memories
Causes the fragile leaves to grow heavy with color
I stand bathed in their iniquities
Captured by the fears I once fought, but can't remember

The boughs of the trees wax and wane
Burdened by the weight of my mind,
Bending to the precipice, where dreams kiss reality's soft lips

This is not the first time
I have seen your ghost amidst the fog
That hangs here in the brisk mornings,

Once as intimate as the droplets of water
That hang in this cloud.
I have stood here amongst the stones
And read their names but
Yours is the only one that amnesia eludes.

You haunt me,
The way your kiss haunted my lips when we parted
The way your memory fades,
Leaving me with nothing but the betrayal of cheeks brushed red
Bound by the chains of your broken promise planted in my heart
Rooted like the trees that have become my cage.

Poem continues ...

Haunted, continued.

Today is the only day I will see you
Where solar and satellite meet in the middle
And the guiltless and the malevolent stand on equal footing.
When you walk away without leaving a part of yourself,
I will remain here seated upon this rock,
Watching as they leave more stones here as memorials of other lost names,
Waiting for the next frigid wind to blow after the long solstice
When you will come and haunt me again like a rainy gloom
That softens your forgotten memories.
Memories that I keep forgetting to forget.

Dedications

"Do I return your precious dreams
after you stole away my own?"

~Chris Wolfe, *Stolen*

A Vendetta with Keats

So who died and made you king of the Romantics?
Well, now that I think about it, I guess you did.
And at a ripe young age too.
It's a shame you died so suddenly,
But that doesn't mean you can come back
And haunt other young poets.
It seems that in recent times
You are in some way involved
In the depressing events and hardest moments.

Keats, you cause mental breakdowns
And frowns, and sometimes your archaic language
makes me sick … with jealousy.
Why is it that you sit there and stare
At mud and clay and see these five-minute epics?
Don't you know that urn has caused tears to fall
Because of your wordy descriptions …
Tears of joyful beauty and tears of sadness because
We can't put down on paper what
The Greek did with dirt.

I should be clear that I despise you. Praise you.
Study you. Reflect you.
And you see, this is the problem.
Because sometimes I wonder if you're trying to
Relive your old days.
I see my own Fanny Brawne, Grecian Urns, and Bright Stars.
Declarations by words
When I don't have the money
To see them through.
You've caused me troubles,
Caused me to feel like I can't breathe.

Poem continues …

A Vendetta with Keats, continued.

So Keats, we're cool for now.
Because we're not so different, you and I.
But should I die next year
Out of some twisted emulation
Of your own life,
Then I know two poets who are going to have words
In the afterlife.

Keats Redux

Nearly 200 years after you died, and you still
Haunt the hearts of poets. At least twice
You've tried to live your life through my own.
Do you haunt every hopeless Romantic seeking after
Their own Ms. Brawne?

Your apparition acts to sway me from my
Bright Star, Diamond in the night sky.

My empathy catches your late wanderings
Writing new streams of creativity to discover.
I, your modern-day scribe, transforming
Archaic quill pen scribblings into constant
Finger-tapped digital intangible.

Your Grecian dirt-clod observations bring
tears to over-pressured diamonds.

For three months leading into my 24th year,
I felt your consumption: spitting out poetic
Life blood and breathing like underwater.
I wondered if you were going to repeat your
Tragic fate just centuries later.

Your blackbird works to take me
Away from my life's potential.

If I am meant to be this generation's Keats,
Then death still only brings success to the name
No one knows while it still has breath. Even for this,
I will continue to write.

Appendix

"You are a thousand paper cranes,
Yet it is the tape that holds you together."
~Chris Wolfe, *Digital Origami*

Thrift Store

I have a job.

Every day I stand at the counter and watch as people sort through racks looking for new skins.

A man comes up to me with two feet and asks, 'how much?'
I tell him, '50 cents.'
He gives me two quarters and walks out of the store.

A woman drops two used hands on the counter.
They were once used by a man.
You can tell by the calluses on the insides.
She asks me, 'how much?' and I tell her 'we give those away.'

After lunch, a woman steps up with a face in her hands.
She hopes that once she gets home, she can throw away the old with the mistakes stapled to it
and she can begin a new life without having to buy one.
We sell those, too.

By the end of the day, I close up and count out the register.
We have made a few eyes and ears today.
It has been a good day.

I have a job.
It is the only place where I kinda hope we close this place down one day.
Not because of bankruptcy but because we've finally given people happy lives
and no one needs to come in here
to buy anything else to make them happy because they already are.

Just because I am an employee doesn't mean I'm not a customer.
Sometimes I wish I could come in here and buy a new face.
Maybe some new hands too.

Poem continues ...

Thrift Store, continued.

Lord knows I need a new ribcage
because this one has too many books in it already.
I'm having to turn them sideways and fit them inside the cracks.

I might just buy a new heart one day.
I have given this one to you already.
Keep it safe until I return.
Hold it a little tighter.

Ink

The tattoo on my wrist is a shadow of something inside me.
The glow within me projects it onto the inside of my skin.
I want to pull it up over me like a blanket.

Writer's Block

Indestructible steel wall built by haystacks and duct tape.
Seventy stories high by one inch wide.
Blueprinted and contracted out by a million and oneself.

What breaks down this wall?
Dynamite, Sledgehammers and Bulldozers?
Wind, rain, and years of erosion?
Do I have the patience to wait that long?
No. The answer was simple.

What breaks down the wall?
A graceful five-foot-six girl
Who simply knocks and crumbles metal frames
Speaks diamonds and doesn't know her own strength.

What breaks down the wall?
A half-broken heart for a lost and found friend
Juggling hearts and minds like bowling pins
And dropping them like a three-ring reject.

What breaks down the wall?
Close goes far away. Distance gains ground.
Misguided intention and internal miscommunication
Truth becomes the result of time and forgiveness

What breaks down the wall?
You do. Thank you.

www.ingramcontent.com/pod-product-compliance
Lightning Source LLC
Chambersburg PA
CBHW060502110426
42738CB00055B/2588